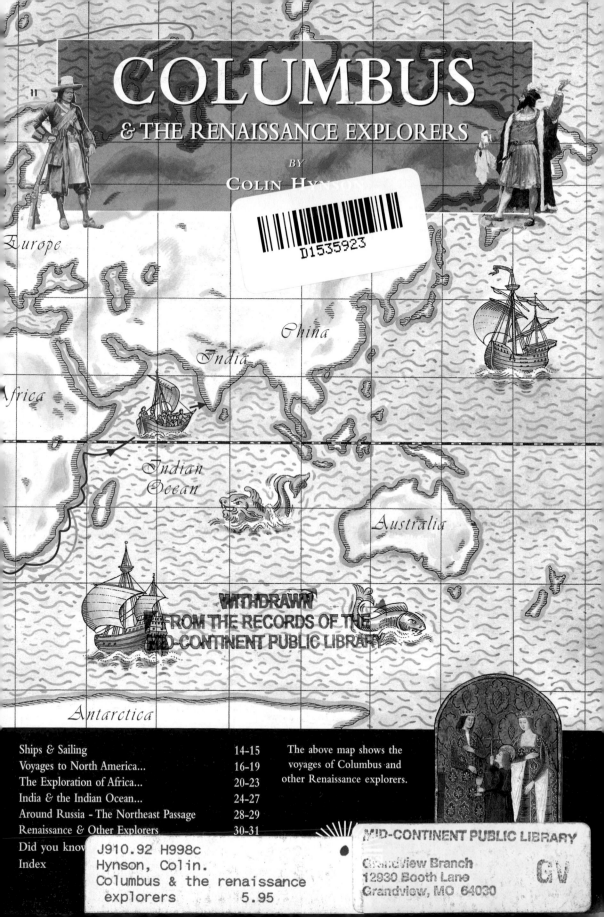

# COLUMBUS
## & THE RENAISSANCE EXPLORERS

*BY*
Colin Hynson

Europe

China

India

Africa

Indian Ocean

Australia

Antarctica

The above map shows the
voyages of Columbus and
other Renaissance explorers.

# The Medieval View of the World

The people of medieval Europe had a very different view than we do about the rest of the world. They did not have the benefit of newspapers, telephones, or television, so news rarely reached ordinary people. Unlike today, they were not able to fly from one continent to another. In fact, very few people went further than the nearest town during their entire lives. However, the way that medieval Europe looked at the world was to be changed forever by two explorers: Christopher Columbus, who sailed westward and found a new world in the Americas, and Vasco da Gama, who sailed eastward and found a sea route to Asia.

## THE MEDIEVAL CHURCH

The Christian people of medieval Europe were unified by a single religious belief. Everybody, from kings to peasants, was a member of the Roman Catholic Church. Although Catholics fought against each other, they all had a common hatred of non-Christians. The Roman Catholic Church believed that it had both a right and a duty to conquer and convert all nonbelievers.

## THE CRUSADES

The Crusades started in 1095 when Pope Urban II urged all Christians to fight the Muslims and capture the holy city of Jerusalem. The First Crusade conquered Jerusalem in 1099 but the Muslims took it back soon afterwards. There were six more unsuccessful Crusades between 1099 and 1250.

## STORIES OF STRANGE CREATURES

Because many Europeans did not know about the people who lived in distant lands, there were many stories about strange and fantastic creatures who lived there. It was believed that there were people with the faces of dogs, people without heads and with their faces on their chests, and giants with only one eye in the middle of their forehead living in foreign lands.

## TRADE IN SPICES

Along with silk, the most important items traded between Asia and Europe were spices, such as nutmeg, shown here. Spices were important because medieval people had to eat meat that was either going rotten or had been preserved with salt. The spices helped to disguise the putrid taste and extreme saltiness of the meat.

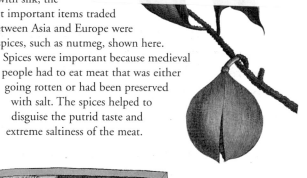

~1441~
*The first African slaves arrive in Portugal.*

~1445~
*The Portuguese sail around Cape Verde, the western tip of West Africa.*

~c.1451~
*Christopher Columbus born in Genoa.*

~1460~
*Prince Henry the Navigator dies.*

## A VIEW OF THE WORLD

This map was first produced in 1482 and is called Ptolemy's world map. It shows how little of the world Europeans really knew about. Southern Africa, the Pacific, and the American continent are not included and Asia seems to be a matter of guesswork. Only the mapping of the Mediterranean is accurate. Even the outlines of Scotland and Ireland look strange to modern eyes.

## SILK

The trade in silk between Asia and Europe was very important but it was also very expensive. The silk had to come to Europe by land through Muslim traders who controlled the trade between the two continents. Demand for silk among the wealthy was very high, creating vast profits for the traders.

## MARCO POLO

Some Europeans traveled long distances. Marco Polo set off for China in 1271 and arrived there more than three years later. He returned to Europe in 1295. His stories of China caught the imaginations of later explorers although many people thought that some of his stories were untrue.

## SIR JOHN MANDEVILLE

Some people wrote fictional travel stories full of wild exaggerations. In the 1350s, a book called *The Travels of Sir John Mandeville* appeared. It was this book that created many of the strange people that Europeans believed existed. One such traveler claimed he met people with giant feet that they used as a shelter from the sun.

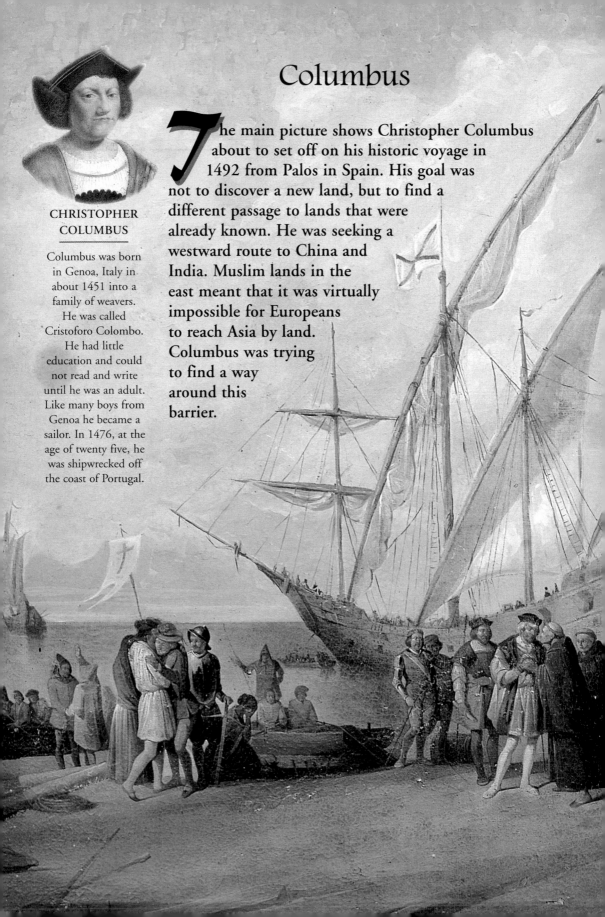

# Columbus

## CHRISTOPHER COLUMBUS

Columbus was born in Genoa, Italy in about 1451 into a family of weavers. He was called Cristoforo Colombo. He had little education and could not read and write until he was an adult. Like many boys from Genoa he became a sailor. In 1476, at the age of twenty five, he was shipwrecked off the coast of Portugal.

The main picture shows Christopher Columbus about to set off on his historic voyage in 1492 from Palos in Spain. His goal was not to discover a new land, but to find a different passage to lands that were already known. He was seeking a westward route to China and India. Muslim lands in the east meant that it was virtually impossible for Europeans to reach Asia by land. Columbus was trying to find a way around this barrier.

## EXPERIENCE IN SAILING

After his shipwreck, Columbus stayed on in Portugal and settled in Lisbon. He married, learned to become a mapmaker, and continued his career as a sailor. He visited the West African coast, England, and Ireland. He later claimed that he also sailed to Iceland.

## THE WEALTH OF THE INDIES

Columbus called his plan *"the enterprise of the Indies."* When medieval Europeans used the word "Indies" they did not mean just India, but also Japan, China, Indonesia, and Southeast Asia. It was believed that these were all very wealthy lands. Using Marco Polo's calculations, Columbus worked out that India was about 3,900 miles west of Europe. In fact, this is more or less the distance between Europe and the American coast.

## KING JOHN II OF PORTUGAL

It was while he was sailing in the Atlantic that Columbus deduced it might be possible to sail westward from Europe to Asia. He first asked King John II of Portugal for help in 1484, but he was refused. The Portuguese were looking for a route to Asia around the African coast.

## THE SPANISH INQUISITION

The inquisition punished anybody who strayed from Roman Catholic teaching. Torture was used to obtain confessions and the guilty were often burned alive. In Spain the inquisition was used mostly against Jews, who were forced to convert to Christianity. Jews who refused to convert were ordered out of Spain on August 3, 1492, the day Columbus began his voyage across the Atlantic.

## CHRISTOPHER COLUMBUS
### -A Time Line-

~c.1460~

*Vasco da Gama born.*

~1476~

*Columbus is shipwrecked off Portugal and starts to work for the Portuguese.*

~1482~

*Diogo Cao sails further along the West African coast than any other European.*

~1484~

*King John II of Portugal turns down Columbus's request for help to sail west.*

~1485~

*Columbus moves to Spain to look for help from King Ferdinand and Queen Isabella.*

## HERNANDO DE TALAVERA

The King and Queen of Spain set up a special commission of priests, astrologers, and scholars to look at Columbus's proposals. It was headed by Hernando de Talavera, who was a monk and Queen Isabella's confessor. This church was named after him. The commission took until 1490 to come to a conclusion and it advised the monarchs to reject Columbus's plan.

## FERDINAND AND ISABELLA

Spain was divided into several kingdoms, the two largest being Castile and Aragon. The heir to the throne of Castile, Isabella, married the heir to the throne of Aragon, Ferdinand. When they became monarchs of their kingdoms, the two thrones ruled together. A unified Spain, under Isabella I and Ferdinand II, was now much stronger.

## SANTANGEL THE TREASURER

Columbus needed friends at the royal court to present his case to the king and queen. One of his major supporters was Santangel the Treasurer, who looked after the finances of the two monarchs. Without his support, Columbus's plan would have been rejected.

# The Court of Ferdinand and Isabella

The refusal of King John II of Portugal to fund Columbus's plan to sail across the Atlantic to the Indies must have been a terrible blow to him. One year after John II had turned him down, Columbus decided to move with his family to Spain, to see if he could get support for his voyage there. A great deal of rivalry existed between Spain and Portugal, particularly over finding a sea route to Asia. Columbus hoped to use this rivalry to convince the Spanish to support him and so have the advantage over the Portuguese. However, Columbus's plan to find a westward route to Asia seemed incredible to many people. Ferdinand and Isabella had to be convinced to finance a very risky venture.

## THE NEED FOR GOLD

It was Ferdinand and Isabella's constant need for gold, even more than spices or silks, that made them finally accept Columbus's plan. The costs of waging war against the Moors and the expense of their magnificent court meant that they were very short of money.

## THE RECONQUISTA

In the eighth century most of Spain was conquered by the Moors, Muslims from North Africa. The Spanish dreamed of driving them out and making Spain a Christian country again. Under Ferdinand and Isabella the Reconquista (the "Reconquest") began, and by 1492 the Moors were finally pushed out of Spain, seven hundred years after they had first arrived.

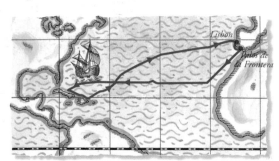

*Columbus's 1st voyage* ———

# Columbus's First Voyage

I t took another two years for Ferdinand and Isabella to accept Talavera's recommendations and turn down Columbus's proposals. He was extremely disappointed. He was contemplating approaching the king of France when he met a new ally, a ship owner named Martin Alonso Pinzon. Columbus returned with his new partner and asked again for royal support. He also demanded that he be made governor of any new lands he found and granted 10 percent of all the gold, jewels, and spices. Ferdinand and Isabella refused him at first, but he gradually won them over. When he finally received royal approval, Columbus moved quickly. He and Pinzon soon had three ships ready to sail and the journey began at dawn on August 3, 1492.

## DEALING WITH MUTINY

Once the ships were out of sight of land, many of the sailors became nervous. They knew that they would reach land eventually but they were afraid that they might run out of food before then. Columbus prevented the crew from mutinying and forcing the ships to return to Spain by lying to them about how close they were to land.

## LAND SIGHTED AT LAST

After several false alarms, land was finally sighted by a member of Columbus's crew on October 12, 1492, more than two months after they had set off from Spain. The land found was one of the islands of the modern Bahamas. Columbus named it San Salvador. The local population were called Arawaks but Columbus was convinced that he had arrived at the Indies and so he called them Indians.

## SIGHTING OF A VOLCANO

After sailing from Spain, the ships landed at the Canary Islands to take on new supplies. While Columbus was there a live volcano near Tenerife erupted on August 24, 1492. According to his journal, many of the crew, who were already nervous about the voyage, were frightened by the eruption. Columbus tried to explain what volcanoes were to the Spanish sailors.

## THE SHIPS ON THE VOYAGE

Columbus took three ships on his journey across the Atlantic. They were the *Pinta*, the *Niña* (captained by Pinzon and his brother) and Columbus's own ship the *Santa Maria*. The *Santa Maria* was just over 100 feet long (around fifty-five meters) with the others just half that length. The total crew for these three ships numbered ninety men.

## RETURN TO SPAIN

When Columbus left Hispaniola, he left thirty-eight men behind and enough food and ammunition for a year. He and his crew moved on to the *Niña* and sailed for Spain on January 4, 1493. The *Pinta* joined the *Niña* on January 6. Eventually he arrived at the Azores on February 18 and Portugal on March 4. Columbus then sailed to Palos on March 15 and went to meet the king and queen at Barcelona in triumph.

## CUBA AND ONWARD

After leaving San Salvador, Columbus arrived at Cuba. He was convinced that he had arrived in China and sent off a team to find the "Great Khan." They came back after finding nothing. The ships then sailed to Haiti, which Columbus named Hispaniola (the "Spanish Island"). According to the first published account of the people of the New World, in 1497, they lived to 150, had no government, and ate human flesh.

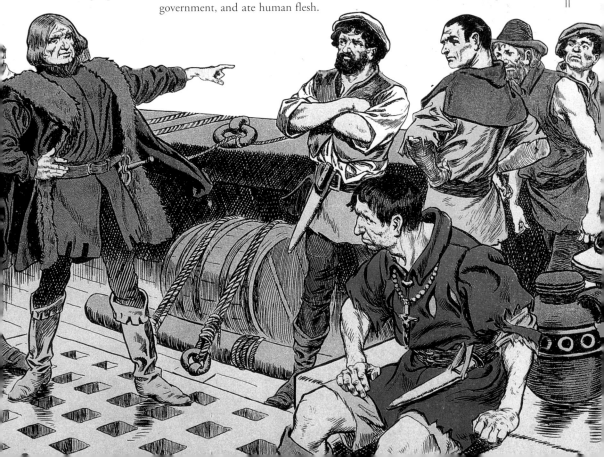

## A NEW CONTINENT

During Columbus's later voyages it became clear that he had not found a new route to the Indies. Instead, he had discovered a continent unknown to the Europeans. After meeting natives in Venezuela on his third journey, in 1498, he wrote in his journal that he had found *"a very great continent...where Christianity will have so much enjoyment and our faith in time so great an increase."*

## SHIPS FOR LATER VOYAGES

While Columbus had only three ships on his first voyage, things were very different for his second. Ferdinand and Isabella were so determined that Spain should stay in control of what they thought was the westward route to Asia that they gave Columbus seventeen ships. The fact that his third voyage had only six ships and his fourth voyage had just four, shows how much Columbus fell from favor with Ferdinand and Isabella.

## CHRISTOPHER COLUMBUS
### -A TIME LINE-

*~1488~*

*The Cape of Good Hope reached by Bartolomeu Diaz.*

*~1490~*

*The commission under Talavera recommends that the Spanish royal family turn down Columbus's proposals.*

*~1492~*

*Christopher Columbus sets off on his first voyage and lands at San Salvador.*

*~1493~*

*Christopher Columbus returns to Spain and sets off on his second voyage.*

## THE DISCOVERY OF VENEZUELA

Columbus set off on his third voyage on May 30, 1498. He was searching for the mainland that he believed should have been near the islands that he had discovered. After discovering the island of Trinidad in July 1498, he sailed to the coast of South America. On August 5, 1498, he landed on the coast of Venezuela and became the first European to set foot in South America. He also sighted the Orinoco River, which runs between Venezuela and Brazil. Columbus believed that Venezuela was part of an island and that Cuba was part of the mainland.

# Columbus's Later Voyages

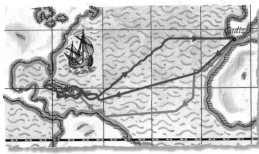

**W**hen Columbus arrived at the royal court in Barcelona he was received by Ferdinand and Isabella with a great deal of honor.

Columbus had brought back some gold, amber, and an escort of Indians. Both monarchs were convinced that Columbus had reached the Indies. He was made Governor of the Indies and Admiral of the Ocean Sea. He was urged to go on another expedition as soon as possible to explore and colonize the lands. Ferdinand and Isabella were concerned that the Portuguese would send their own ships and claim the land as theirs, so Columbus went on another three journeys across the Atlantic, but none of them was as successful as the first.

*Columbus's 2nd voyage* —— *3rd voyage* ——

## COLUMBUS AS GOVERNOR

On his second voyage Columbus returned to Navidad and found that the whole camp had been destroyed and the Spaniards killed. He ordered that a new colony called Isabella be built. In April 1494, he left to explore Cuba and Jamaica and returned to Isabela five months later as Governor of the Indies. He was not a good governor. He argued with the Spanish nobles and administrators sent by Ferdinand and Isabella. He returned to Spain in June 1496 with none of the riches that he had promised the two monarchs.

### SHIPWRECKED OFF JAMAICA

His fourth and last voyage in 1502 was perhaps his most difficult. He had to pay for the voyage himself. After dealing with a mutiny by his crew, a storm nearly destroyed his ships and he was shipwrecked on Jamaica for a year.

# Columbus's Later Voyages

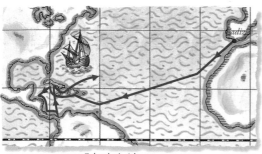

Columbus's 4th voyage ———

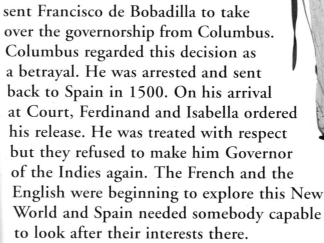

Columbus gradually fell from favor at the Spanish Court when his subsequent voyages proved less fruitful than the first. The king and queen remained loyal to him but they realized that, while he was a great explorer, he was not competent as a governor. During his third voyage in 1498 he found the colonists left behind from a previous trip were fighting among themselves. The two monarchs sent Francisco de Bobadilla to take over the governorship from Columbus. Columbus regarded this decision as a betrayal. He was arrested and sent back to Spain in 1500. On his arrival at Court, Ferdinand and Isabella ordered his release. He was treated with respect but they refused to make him Governor of the Indies again. The French and the English were beginning to explore this New World and Spain needed somebody capable to look after their interests there.

### THE NEED FOR GOLD

The lack of gold brought back from Columbus's expeditions proved to be his actual downfall. He failed to convince his royal supporters that he had indeed discovered a new route to Asia. His later voyages were also marred by ill-disciplined and gold-hungry crews.

### VISITING THE MAINLAND

Columbus rarely visited the mainland of the American continent. It was only on his third voyage that he eventually landed at Venezuela in South America. On his fourth voyage he explored the coast of Central America. He visited the Gulf of Mexico and the coasts of Honduras, Nicaragua, Costa Rica (shown here), and Panama. He was still looking for a sea route to the Indies.

## THE DEATH OF COLUMBUS

Columbus returned to Spain after his fourth and final
ourney in November 1504. By this time he was very
ill and he had to be carried to Seville. After Queen
Isabella died, he was taken to see Ferdinand.
Columbus said that he should be given back the
governorship of the Indies. After Ferdinand
refused, Columbus's health got worse.
He wrote his will on May 19, 1506,
and died the next day at Valladolid,
in Spain, a disappointed man
abandoned by his monarchs.

## COLUMBUS'S SHIPS

On all of his voyages Columbus depended on a particular type of
ship called the caravel. These were ships that normally weighed
about 50 tons and had a crew of about twenty. They had
two masts. Their triangular sails made them easy to
maneuver and because they were not as heavy as
other ships they could be used in shallow water
such as along coastlines. This made them ideal
for exploration. However, their small size was
also a disadvantage. It meant that they
could carry only limited amounts of
food, water, and
other supplies. On long
journeys, a constant
problem was the ability to
carry sufficient food and water
for the duration of the voyage.
Gradually explorers began to use
larger vessels called "carracks" to
carry their provisions.

## DIEGO COLUMBUS

Several members of the
Columbus family took part in
the early voyages. His brother, Bartolomé, was in charge of the colony of
Isabella during his second voyage. Columbus's eldest son, Diego (on the
left of the picture), served as a page to Prince Juan, heir to the two
thrones of Spain. When Columbus died, Diego was named Admiral
of the Indies and Governor of Hispaniola. He continued to claim all
of the privileges that Ferdinand and Isabella first gave to his father.
He was not successful.

# Ships & Sailing

The crews of the early voyages of exploration faced many dangers. Not only did they have to put up with cramped conditions and only a small supply of food and water (which was often bad), but they were sailing into the unknown with little idea where they were and how fast they were traveling. Perhaps it is not surprising therefore that Columbus and others often had to face mutiny. Today ships have little trouble locating their exact position. Accurate maps, clocks, and even global positioning satellites mean that sailors can tell where they are to within a few feet. Sailors in the 15th and 16th centuries were not so fortunate.

## MAGNETIC COMPASS

It was vitally important that the sailors crossing the Atlantic knew exactly in what direction they were sailing. On a clear day or night either the sun or the North Star was used. They could also use a magnetic compass. The magnetic field around the earth caused a magnetized needle floating in water to always point northward.

## DEAD RECKONING

If a navigator knew where his ship sailed from, what its speed was, the direction the ship was traveling in, and how long they had been traveling, then it was possible to calculate how far they had traveled by "dead reckoning" and so find their position. However, winds and tides meant that this was only an approximate way of working out the ship's position. Columbus was regarded as a great navigator because of his skill with "dead reckoning."

## THE ASTROLABE

Every navigator in Columbus's time made use of the astrolabe (similar to this "Arabic" example). It could be used for finding out how far north or south of the equator (latitude) the ship was. It worked by measuring the height of the North Star or noon sun from the ship. Once the height was known then the navigator could calculate how far north or south he was.

## THE CROSS STAFF

The simplest way to measure the
latitude of a ship was to use an
instrument called a cross staff.
It had a crossbar for sighting
and a rod with measurements cut into
the side. The crossbar would be lined up
between the sun or North Star and the horizon.
The measurements of the long piece of wood
would then tell the navigator the angle of
the sun or star from the horizon. From this
he could work out his latitude. There is
considerable danger in staring at the sun
for too long. In 1595 Captain John
Davis invented the backstaff, which
used mirrors and shadows so that
navigators did not risk being injured.

## TELLING THE TIME

For the navigator
to calculate a ship's
position, it was vital
that he knew what time
of day it was. Sailors
would be given the job of
watching a large sand-filled
hour-glass (similar to this
17th-century example, shown here).
It normally emptied after thirty
minutes and then a bell would be rung so
that everybody on board knew what the time was.

## THE QUADRANT

Alongside the astrolabe it is likely that Columbus took some
quadrants with him. When Ferdinand Magellan started on
his famous voyage around the world in 1519, he took
seven astrolabes and twenty one quadrants. Quadrants
did basically the same job as astrolabes.
They worked by lining up one arm with
the horizon and then moving a movable arm
so that it was pointing at either the sun or
North Star. The angle between these two
arms could then be used to calculate the
ship's latitude. It could only really work
when the sea was calm and still.

## JOHN CABOT

Henry VII of England heard of Columbus's discoveries and approached John Cabot, who claimed that he could reach Asia across the North Atlantic. On his first voyage in 1497 he reached Canada and returned to a hero's welcome. However, Cabot and all of his crew disappeared without a trace during their second voyage in 1498.

## THE NORTHWEST PASSAGE

Once it was realized that this land was not Asia but a new continent, explorers wanted to find a way around it. After Ferdinand Magellan found a way around the southern tip of America, the French and English looked for a route through northern waters.

## CHRISTOPHER COLUMBUS
### -A Time Line-

*~1494~*
*Treaty of Tordesillas between Spain and Portugal signed, dividing the non-Christian world between them.*

*~1497~*
*Vasco da Gama sets sail for the Indies.*

*John Cabot sets sail from England to find a new route to Asia.*

*Columbus begins his third voyage.*

*~1498~*
*Vasco da Gama arrives in India.*

## THE INUIT

The natives that Frobisher met in Canada called themselves Inuit. This translates into English as "people." Those who lived south of the Inuit called them Eskimos, which means "eaters of raw meat." Frobisher regarded them as savages but they had devised a way of living in one of the harshest places known.

## SAILING INTO DANGER

Explorers searching for the Northwest Passage soon discovered the dangers of such a voyage. The further north they went the colder the climate became. Rope and sails would freeze and there was the constant danger of icebergs or being stuck fast in an icesheet.

## FIGHTING THE INUIT

Frobisher's crew fought with the Inuit, who had kidnapped five of the crew. He decided to capture an Inuit in a kayak. He drew him to his ship by ringing a bell over the side and then suddenly grabbing him. On his return to England both the unfortunate Inuit and his kayak were presented to the king.

# Voyages to North America...

ne of the reasons why Ferdinand and Isabella were not anxious to allow Christopher Columbus to remain as governor of the newly discovered lands was the threat from other European powers, particularly France and England. The Spanish believed that the French and English would try to take the land away for

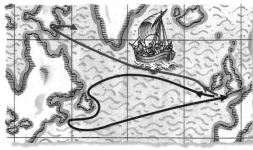

*Frobisher* ══════ *Cabot* ═════

themselves, so they sent ships and weapons and set up colonies with strong governors. It worked too well. The French and English explorers simply ignored the parts of America that the Spanish had conquered. It would have been too costly in terms of money and lives to attempt to overthrow them. Instead they turned their attention to the unexplored lands of North America and Canada.

### SIR MARTIN FROBISHER

This picture shows Sir Martin Frobisher's crew fighting with the Inuit in Canada. Frobisher had sailed to Canada looking for the northwest passage to Asia. He set off from London in June 1576 with three ships. One ship sank off Greenland and another turned back after the crew mutinied. Frobisher sailed on and reached Baffin Island. He too thought, mistakenly, that he had found the route through to Asia.

# ...Voyages to North America

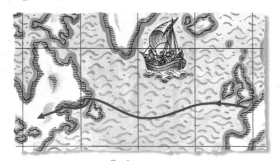

*Cartier* ━━━

The Spanish and Portuguese soon realized that the lands that they had discovered were not the Indies, and that it would be very difficult to sail around South America to Asia. They began to look for any wealth that they could find in their new lands. French and English explorers also started to search for riches in North America and Canada. Like the Spaniards and Portuguese, they were looking for gold. The French explorer, Jacques Cartier, sailed along the coast of Canada searching for the Northwest Passage. He abandoned this search when local people, the Hurons, told him of land to the west full of gold and rubies. He set off inland to find it but was unsuccessful.

## TRADING IN FUR

The French exploration of Canada became dominated by the fur trade from animals such as the beaver and the elk. The Canadian Indians were essential to this trade as trackers and guides. In return, they were given alcohol and guns, which they used to fight among themselves. The English explorers were less interested in the fur trade and began instead to start exploiting the oceans surrounding Canada. John Cabot reported that he found schools of fish so big that they slowed his ship down. Canadian fish became a common food in England.

## FOOL'S GOLD

When Sir Martin Frobisher arrived at Baffin Island, he found pieces of black rock that he thought might be gold. He returned in 1577 and collected 200 tons. A year later he went on a third trip, taking thirty tin miners from Cornwall with him. With the backing of rich investors, he took fifteen ships on the voyage. Frobisher came home with 1000 tons of the rock, but what he had found was iron pyrite, known as "fool's gold." Frobisher was ruined and the investors lost all their money.

## COLONIZATION

Like the Spanish and the Portuguese, the English and French authorities began to realize that they could only really hold on to the land they had discovered by establishing colonies. These new colonies depended on the trade created by the explorers. Early French settlements like Port Royal in Nova Scotia and Quebec were based entirely on the fur trade. The English built settlements in Newfoundland in order to salt and pack cod destined for English tables.

## CHRISTOPHER COLUMBUS
### -A Time Line-

-1498-
*John Cabot sets off on his second voyage.*

-1499-
*Vasco da Gama returns to Portugal.*

-1500-
*Brazil discovered by Pedro Cabral.*

*Columbus arrested and sent back to Spain.*

-1502-
*Da Gamsa makes a second voyage to India to avenge the massacre of Portuguese in Calicut.*

## FINDING THE NORTHWEST PASSAGE

Terrible sailing conditions were not the only reason why several English and French explorers were discouraged in their quest to find the Northwest Passage. On several occasions they sailed into large inlets, which they thought were ways through to the Pacific Ocean and Asia. Jacques Cartier sailed into the mouth of the St. Lawrence River and thought he had found a route through America. So did Sir Martin Frobisher in 1576 when he sailed on alone and discovered Frobisher Bay on Baffin Island. The Northwest Passage was not successfully negotiated until 1903.

# The Exploration of Africa...

*Lisbon*

*Diaz* ——

**P**ortugal and Spain had been conquered by the Moors in the 7th century. Portugal finally threw out the Islamic invaders in 1249 and King John I of Portugal went on to conquer part of Morocco. Portugal's position on the Atlantic coastline made it ideally placed for overseas exploration and Portuguese mariners began to look for a way to the Indies around Africa. By 1419 they had reached Madeira and in 1431 they sailed to the Azores. In 1445 Portuguese sailors had gone around Cape Verde, the western tip of West Africa. By 1482 they crossed the equator and had reached the mouth of the Congo River.

## ENCOUNTERS WITH AFRICAN

When the Portuguese sailors came into contact with the people who lived in Africa they must have been amazed by their culture and appearance. Sculpture like this brass figure made by a member of the Asante people, who came from modern-day Ghana, would have looked very strange indeed. The Africans must also have been astonished by the Portuguese sailors when they first appeared off the coast in their tall ship

## PRINCE HENRY THE NAVIGATOR

Prince Henry the Navigator was the third son of John I. He spent his life studying navigation and directed the Portuguese exploration of the West African coast. He was a devout Christian who wanted to launch a crusade to drive the Muslims out of North Africa. Finding a way to Asia would help to pay for this crusade and at the same time would weaken the hold that the Muslims had over the trade in gold and spices between Europe and Asia.

## THE LEGEND OF PRESTER JOHN

One of the ways that Henry the Navigator hoped to destroy Muslim North Africa was to find Prester John. From the crusades onwards, there were stories in Europe of a legendary Christian king called Prester John who ruled a kingdom somewhere in Africa. There were other stories that placed his kingdom in South Asia.

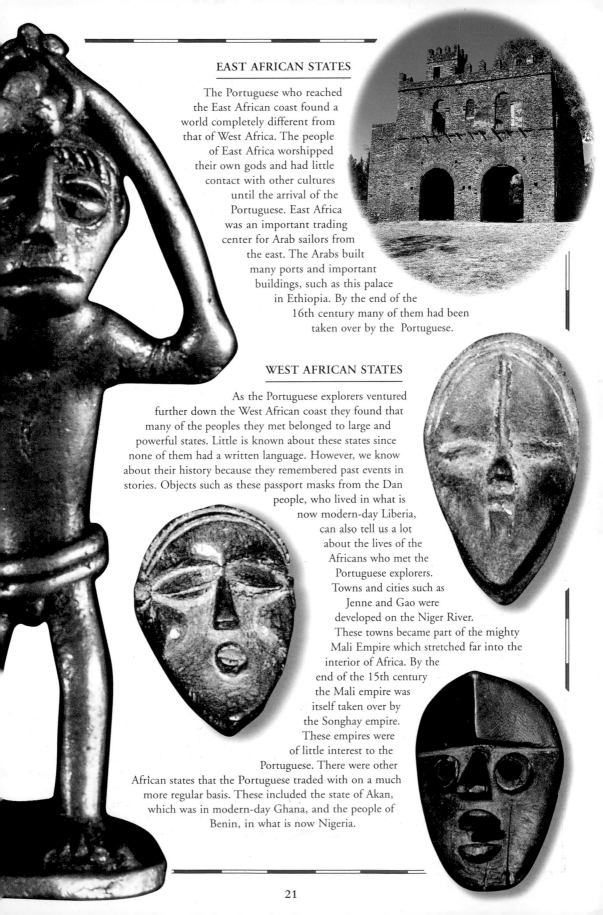

## EAST AFRICAN STATES

The Portuguese who reached the East African coast found a world completely different from that of West Africa. The people of East Africa worshipped their own gods and had little contact with other cultures until the arrival of the Portuguese. East Africa was an important trading center for Arab sailors from the east. The Arabs built many ports and important buildings, such as this palace in Ethiopia. By the end of the 16th century many of them had been taken over by the Portuguese.

## WEST AFRICAN STATES

As the Portuguese explorers ventured further down the West African coast they found that many of the peoples they met belonged to large and powerful states. Little is known about these states since none of them had a written language. However, we know about their history because they remembered past events in stories. Objects such as these passport masks from the Dan people, who lived in what is now modern-day Liberia, can also tell us a lot about the lives of the Africans who met the Portuguese explorers. Towns and cities such as Jenne and Gao were developed on the Niger River. These towns became part of the mighty Mali Empire which stretched far into the interior of Africa. By the end of the 15th century the Mali empire was itself taken over by the Songhay empire. These empires were of little interest to the Portuguese. There were other African states that the Portuguese traded with on a much more regular basis. These included the state of Akan, which was in modern-day Ghana, and the people of Benin, in what is now Nigeria.

# ...The Exploration of Africa

The Portuguese were not interested in exploring the interior of Africa. They traded with the peoples they encountered, but they were looking for a sea route to the Indies. However, they knew that places on the coast of Africa were important landing stages for ships. The route around Africa to Asia took many years to discover. In 1482 King John II sent Diogo Cao to find the Indies. He did not find it but he did discover that Africa was much larger than many people thought. It was Bartolmeo Diaz in 1488 who finally sailed around the southern tip of Africa. He followed the coast of Africa and sailed further south than any other European had managed until then.

## BARTOLMEO DIAZ

Diaz's ships were driven out of sight of land by a fierce storm. When it became calm he sailed north and found that the coast was now on his left and not on his right as expected. He had sailed around the southern tip of Africa by accident.

## BUILDING IN AFRICA

The Portuguese did not explore the interior of Africa and they decided not to establish any African colonies at this stage. However, they knew they had to protect their trade routes to Asia so they built a series of forts along the coastline. They could supply and protect Portuguese ships and keep out foreign competitors.

## TRADING WITH AFRICANS

The two things that the Portuguese wanted when trading with the Akan and Benin peoples were gold and slaves. The Akan supplied most of West Africa's gold, which came from rivers in the interior of Africa. The Portuguese bought this gold from the Akan with slaves they had either captured themselves or bought from the Benin people. Many slaves were also transported back to Portugal and sold again.

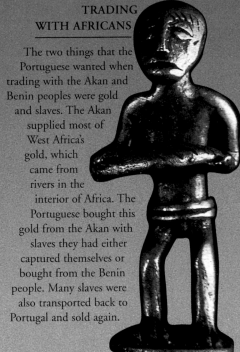

## THE CAPE OF GOOD HOPE

When Bartolmeo Diaz reached the southern tip of Africa he decided to call it "Cabo Tormentoso," which means the Cape of Storms. King John II rejected this name because it was too gloomy and gave it the name Cape of Good Hope, because it raised hopes of eventually reaching the Indies.

## THE RICHES OF THE INDIES

Bartolmeo Diaz was given the task of preparing da Gama's ships for the journey. He loaded them with objects to trade with the Africans such as hawkbells, rings, cloth, and olive oil. It did not occur to him that the rulers of the Indies would not be impressed with these objects. The picture shows how wealthy and abundant in food the Indies were. This cargo was to cause da Gama some problems when he arrived at India.

## DA GAMA'S SHIPS

Da Gama had a fleet of four ships: the *San Gabriel*, the *Sao Rafael*, the *Barrio,* and a storage ship which had no name but had 3 years' supply of food and drink. The ships set off from Lisbon on July 8, 1497. The picture shows the storeship burning. This was done deliberately by da Gama because he was afraid that if the storeship was lost in bad weather then his crew would starve. The supplies were crammed onto the other ships before the empty storeship was set on fire.

## CLAIMING LAND FOR PORTUGAL

Among the stores that da Gama carried on his voyage were stone crosses called padroes. These were set in high ground to act as markers for crews who were to follow them. They were also used when Portugal claimed any newly discovered land. This cross is at Malindi in modern-day Kenya. Da Gama had a difficult time in East Africa because Arab traders did not welcome them there.

# India & the Indian Ocean...

da Gama ━━━ Cabral ━━━

The Portuguese did more than build forts to protect their trade routes to the Indies. In 1494 Spain and Portugal signed the Treaty of Tordesillas which divided the world between the two countries. It gave Spain control over all non-Christian lands west of an imaginary line in the mid-Atlantic. Portugal was given everything to the east. This meant that only the Portuguese could use the route around Africa to Asia. It took ten years from the time Bartolmeo Diaz discovered the way around Africa for Portuguese ships to finally reach India. The new king of Portugal, Manuel I, chose Vasco da Gama to lead this expedition.

## VASCO DA GAMA

Very little is known about Vasco da Gama's early life. He was born sometime in the early 1460s and became a soldier. He also studied navigation from Portuguese sailors. It was this skill together with his military knowledge and qualities as a leader that made him the ideal candidate for Portugal's first expedition to the Indies.

## DEALING WITH MUTINY

King Manuel I had chosen da Gama because he had a reputation for being a good leader and for keeping discipline. At first da Gama had to sail out into the Atlantic to catch the wind that would take him eastward. He was out of sight of land for thirteen weeks. Some of the crew thought they would never see land again. They mutinied and tried to force da Gama to return home, but he convinced them that they would land soon. The ringleaders of the mutiny were arrested and bound in chains.

# ...India & the Indian Ocean

**W**hen da Gama reached the East African port of Malindi he saw four ships that looked strange to him. This was his first contact with Indian traders. The Sultan of Malindi turned out to be friendly and helped da Gama with the rest of his trip. When da Gama set off across the Indian Ocean he had on board a pilot named Ahmed ibn Majid. With his help da Gama managed to sail across the Indian Ocean in only twenty three days. He arrived at Calicut, the main trading city in southern India, on May 20, 1498. The eastward route to Asia had been found.

## BOMBARDING CALICUT

Another explorer, Pedro Cabral, was sent to Calicut after da Gama had returned to Portugal. He set up a trading center at Calicut, left behind some Portuguese traders, and sailed home. Local Muslims attacked the center and killed everybody inside. Da Gama was sent to take revenge. When he reached Calicut in 1502 he bombarded the city with cannon. From then on, the Portuguese controlled the Indian trade routes with military force.

## HINDUS OR CHRISTIANS?

Until da Gama reached India no European had even heard of Hinduism, the main religion of India. When da Gama first saw a Hindu temple he was convinced the people must be Christians. He thought a statue of a goddess, like the one shown, was the Virgin Mary. Images of gods and goddesses painted on the wall seemed to be Christian saints. Da Gama returned to Portugal with tales of Indian Christians.

## RETURN TO PORTUGAL

The picture shows the king of Portugal, Manuel I, greeting da Gama on his return from India.

Da Gama had set off from Calicut on August 29, 1498. He decided to avoid East Africa. Such a long voyage without taking on fresh supplies had a terrible effect on the crew. When he reached Lisbon in September 1499, only fifty-four out of the original crew of 170 were still alive. King Manuel was overjoyed. Portugal had beaten Spain in the race to reach the Indies.

## BUILDING AN EMPIRE

From centers such as Goa and the rebuilt city of Calicut, shown here, the Portuguese began to take control of the rest of the Asian trade routes. They reached China in 1513 and Japan in 1542. The Portuguese knew that many of the spices they found in India came from some islands in Southeast Asia. They decided that they had to control the route to these islands. In 1511 Alfonso de Albuquerque captured the Muslim port of Malacca, which controlled this route. From Malacca, the Portuguese could easily reach the islands that grew spices.

## FIGHTING FOR CONTROL

The Portuguese were determined to take control of trade with India. King Manuel sent two commanders, Alfonso de Albuquerque and Francisco de Almeida, to carry out this task. De Almeida sailed along the East African coast and attacked the Arab traders who had caused da Gama such difficulties. Muslim oared galleys were no match for Portuguese ships, and in the Battle of Diu the entire Muslim fleet was destroyed. Goa was captured by Alfonso de Albuquerque in 1510. He burned the city to the ground and built a new city. The picture shows a Portuguese-style building in Goa.

## ARRIVAL AT CALICUT

The ruler of Calicut was called the Zamorin. When da Gama met the Zamorin he laid out the gifts he had brought with him. The Zamorin was insulted by what he saw as cheap goods and sent da Gama away. Da Gama was allowed to trade but could not compete with the Arab traders. He spent three months in Calicut but managed to buy only a few spices. After a dispute with the Zamorin over taxes da Gama decided to sail for home.

## STUCK IN THE ICE

Willem Barents was a Dutch explorer who was also trying to find a way to Asia around Russia. He made three voyages into the north. During the third voyage his ship became stuck. He was eventually forced to abandon his ship after the ice began to crush it.

## WILLOUGHBY'S FATE

As Willoughby sailed northward a strong wind separated the three ships. Willoughby found one ship but Chancellor's ship had disappeared. He sailed on to Lapland. The weather was getting colder and his ships found it impossible to move as the sea began to freeze. He decided to stop for the winter. The extreme cold and scurvy claimed the lives of Willoughby and all of his crew.

## SAMOYED ARCHERS

Explorers of northern Russia were surprised to find people living in the Arctic. The Samoyed were a nomadic people who moved into the north of Russia during the summer and then, as the winter set in, south to the warmer Russian tundra. They survived by herding nomadic reindeer. It is believed that less than fifty thousand Samoyed are still alive today.

## CHRISTOPHER COLUMBUS
### -A Time Line-

~1534~

*Jacques Cartier tries to find the Northwest Passage.*

~1542~

*The Portuguese reach Japan.*

~1551~

*English merchants form a company to fund an expedition to find the Northeast Passage.*

## FACING DANGER

Explorers looking for the Northeast Passage had to face many of the problems faced by those explorers who were looking for a way to Asia around Canada. During an Arctic winter the sea itself froze and ships could be crushed. In warmer weather loose chunks of ice also posed a threat as did polar bears who were also known to attack sailors.

## BARENTS IN THE WINTER

When Barents and his crew had to abandon their ship they walked across the frozen sea to the island of Novaya Zemlya. They built a shelter from the wood of their ship and spent the winter there. They killed polar bears for their fat which they used in their oil lamps. In the spring they sailed back to Lapland in small lifeboats.

# Around Russia - The Northeast Passage

*Frobisher* ——— *Willoughby* ——— *Barents* ———

It must have seemed to the English that between them Spain and Portugal had taken over the whole of the trade with the east. Da Gama had reached India after voyaging eastward around Africa and Magellan had sailed to Asia from the west in 1520-21. English and French attempts to find a passage across the top of Canada had come to nothing. It was perhaps inevitable that some would search for a route to Asia by sailing through the Arctic and across northern Russia. In late 1551 a group of English merchants formed a company to try to find a new route to Asia. Sebastian Cabot, the son of John Cabot, was made head of the company. The voyage was to be led by Sir Hugh Willoughby. Richard Chancellor was his deputy and was well known as a skilled navigator. The expedition set off on May 10, 1553 from London.

## IVAN THE TERRIBLE

When Richard Chancellor was separated from Willoughby, he continued sailing until he reached the coast of Russia. There he was well treated and taken to Moscow to meet the Tsar of Russia. He was called Ivan the Terrible because of his cruelty to his subjects. However, he treated Chancellor well and held a banquet in his honor. This meeting led to trade between England and Russia. The English exchanged guns and cloth for Russian fur and animal fat.

# Renaissance & Other Explorers

The exploration of the Americas and Asia continued long after they were first encountered by Europeans. The explorers who came after Columbus and da Gama had many reasons for exploring these new-found lands. Sometimes, simply a love of adventure and danger. Many of them, though, hoped to find land and wealth and so make themselves and their monarchs rich men. Others went with a missionary zeal wanting to convert anyone they met to Christianity. Most of the explorers of North America and Canada were either English or French. The exploration of South America and the Indies was left to the Spanish and Portuguese.

## AMERIGO VESPUCCI

Vespucci was an Italian sailor who had a continent named after him. He claimed to have made four voyages to the New World, but only two are certain. His travel writings were very popular and a German mapmaker named the New World map he was making after him "Amerigo," or America.

## WILLIAM DAMPIER

Dampier was born in England in 1651. His early life at sea included a trip to Newfoundland in Canada. In 1698 he led a scientific expedition to lands to the south of Asia that had just been discovered. His voyage took him to the west coast of Australia and the islands of Indonesia.

## HENRY HUDSON

Hudson tried to find the Northeast and Northwest Passages. His first voyage was in 1607 when he tried to find the Northeast Passage but his ship was blocked by ice. During his fourth voyage in 1610 to find the Northwest Passage he was forced to spend the winter in freezing conditions in a bay now named after him. The crew mutinied and set him adrift in a small boat. He was never heard of again.

## THOMAS CAVENDISH

Thomas Cavendish was an English explorer and the third person to sail around the globe. He set off in July 1586 from Plymouth with three ships. He discovered Port Desire in Argentina before sailing through the Strait of Magellan. He attacked Spanish ships and settlements and then sailed across the Pacific. He returned to England in 1588. He died while sailing to China.

Animum fortuna sequatur

## THE SHIP OF JUAN FERNANDEZ

Juan Fernandez was a Spanish navigator and explorer. In 1563 he sailed from Callao in Peru to Valparaiso in Chile, which was considered a daring feat. He went on to discover several Pacific islands in 1574. There is some evidence that he reached Australia and New Zealand in 1576.

## CHRISTOPHER COLUMBUS
### -A Time Line-

*~1553~*

*Sir Hugh Willoughby and Richard Chancellor sail from London to find the Northeast Passage. Willoughby dies and Chancellor meets Ivan the Terrible.*

*~1569~*

*Spain fights a war with Portugal over the Philippines and emerges victorious.*

*~1576~*

*Martin Frobisher looks for the Northwest Passage.*

*~1577~*

*Frobisher begins his second voyage to search for gold.*

*~1578~*

*Frobisher starts his third and last voyage in the quest for gold.*

*~1596~*

*Willem Barents is trapped on Novaya Zemlya while looking for the Northeast Passage.*

*~1608~*

*The French colony of Quebec in Canada founded.*

## SAMUEL DE CHAMPLAIN

Samuel de Champlain was the son of a French naval captain. He traveled to North America and Canada twelve times between 1603–1616. From 1604–1607 he mapped much of the Canadian Atlantic coast. In 1608 he founded the tiny settlement of Quebec, which was to become the capital of French colonists in Canada. He went on to discover the Ottawa River and the Lakes Champlain, Ontario, and Huron.

# DID YOU KNOW?

**How Islam spread within Africa?** In Africa most people followed their own religion and their own customs. However, the part of Africa that lay around the Sahara Desert was dominated by Islam. It was introduced into Africa from two directions. Just south of the Sahara is an area known as the Sahel. For centuries people in the Sahel crossed the Sahara to trade with the Mediterranean. When Islam spread across North Africa in the 7th and 8th centuries, Islam found its way across the desert with the traders. On the East African coast Islam arrived with Arab merchants who sailed down much of the East African coastline.

**What was the first European colony in Asia?** Goa was the first European colony to be established on the Asian continent and it became the Portuguese capital in India. It was also the last part of India to become independent. India achieved independence from Britain in 1947 but Goa was not returned to India until 1961.

**Why the English and the Dutch ignored the Treaty of Tordesillas?** These two countries sent out expeditions and often crossed into areas which, according to the Treaty, belonged to either Spain or Portugal. They could ignore this because the Treaty was put together by Pope Alexander VI for these two Catholic countries. Since the Netherlands and later England were Protestant they claimed that the Treaty did not apply to them.

**How much the European explorers were involved in slavery?** From the 1440s the Portuguese used their expeditions along the West African coast to capture people and to take them back to Portugal to sell as slaves. Europeans felt that slavery was justified because the people they had captured were not Christians. Once they became slaves then they could become Christians. Africans began to fight back once they realized why the Europeans were there. Portuguese traders soon realized that it would be easier to buy slaves from traders in Benin.

**Where Columbus is buried?** Columbus died on May 20, 1506 at his home in Valladolid in Spain. In 1513 his body was moved to a monastery in Seville. In 1542 Columbus's remains crossed the Atlantic Ocean to Hispaniola and he was buried at the cathedral of Santa Maria in Santo Domingo. However, it is also claimed that Columbus's body lies in Havana or the cathedral of Seville.

**How the Portuguese discovered Brazil?** When Vasco da Gama returned to Portugal from the Indies, Pedro Cabral set off from Lisbon with a fleet of thirteen ships in March 1500. Like da Gama, he began by sailing westward. However, he went much further than he intended. On April 22, he sighted the coast of Brazil. After claiming the land for Portugal he set off eastward for the Indies.

First edition for the United States, its territories and dependencies, Canada and the Philippine Republic, published 1998 by Barron's Educational Series, Inc.
Original edition copyright © 1998 by Ticktock Publishing, Ltd.
U.S. edition copyright © 1998 by Barron's Educational Series, Inc.
All rights reserved. No part of this book may be reproduced in any form, by photostat, microfilm, xerography, or any other means, or incorporated into any information retrieval system, electronic or mechanical, without the permission of the copyright owner.

*All inquiries should be addressed to:*
Barron's Educational Series, Inc.
250 Wireless Boulevard
Hauppauge, New York 11788
http://www.barronseduc.com
Library of Congress Catalog Card No. 97-77634
International Standard Book No. 0-7641-0530-2
Printed in Italy